# In Memoriam of a Modest Shame

**Nnaemeka Oruh**

Published in Nigeria by Baron's Café
An imprint of Fairchild Media
Plot 1-4 Adewumi Layout, Akinyemi, Ibadan, Nigeria.
media@fairchildmedia.com.ng
+2348068108018


ISBN 978-958-959--328-8
Cover Design:
Design and Layout: Faloye Oluwasogo Moses

# Dedication

For Justina Ogoloma-Ochia, who gave the final
push.

# Content

I

## Interlude

## Can hope part the curtain of darkness...

## ...and usher in a new dawn?

## Acknowledgement
## About the author

# Introduction

In Memoriam of a Modest Shame is a collection that will expectedly raise questions on the idea of poetry, what it should be, and how it should be done. These were the same questions that came to mind as I read through the collection, because the poems proceed in a direction that is radically different from what I have been used to as a poetry reader and writer myself. Most of the poems are straightforward expressions, and even literal in many places, decrying what is perceivably the numerous troubles and dysfunctions which our immediate society has ever grappled with. In being able to express a clear disapproval of these shades of wrongness that shadow our society, Nnaemeka shows a keen observatory sense and an uninhibited honesty that may well be applauded.

The poems are largely traditional in structure and form, in the way they voice the thoughts that call them forth, and in the associations and influences which can be inferred from their lines. They spare almost nothing in the inclusive scope of their subject matters, from religion through politics, culture, social realities, historical estrangement, domestic abuse, gender; sometimes they are nostalgic of what has been lost—mostly of traditional innocence—as in "Just a Day":

> Give me one day, just one day,
> a day when I dance around in
> circles,
> at the thought of mum,
> preparing ukazi soup with
> achara.
>
> ...
>
> I need a day, but can't find one,
> when I can bask in the
> euphoria of innocence,
> devoid of backroom mockery.
> All I have now,
> is a world that walks on its
> head.

This expression of what is lamentable is the general attitude of the collection, and it is rightly so because to be familiar with the society of the poet, is to be familiar with the daemons which might have haunted these poems off his mind. There is very little that a poetic mind can hold up at a time before imploding, and in most cases the poem becomes a result and a means of healing when this implosion happens; hence, it seems likely that poetry is mostly sourced from the shadows of existence. It does not, however, mean that poetry goes off to correct any social flaws—this is something poetry may not have the ability to do—but the poet speaks out of empathy and then, according to some lines in one of the poems in this collection, because the chick snatched by the hawk must cry out, not for the hawk to let go but for the world to witness its undoing. This obsession with words sets the poet at odd against the society, which plays out in the first lines and the last stanza of "The Poet":

> Words that come from you,
> perverse definition of me,
> a man whose soul you know
> not.
>             ...
>
> Call me madman,
> call me *Jadum*,
> but I'm that seer,
> who converses with gods,
> in esoteric languages,
> incomprehensible to mere
> mortals.

For all its gloominess, Nnaemeka does not lose track with hope, somehow he finds a way to moor on a bright shore because, perhaps, this is the only way to exist amidst a tumultuous sea. The last two poems in the collection, under "**...and usher in a new dawn?**" calls up a strong resistance to the troubles which are unavoidable in existence. Everything— present struggle and protest—is rounded up in "Revolution":

> But tomorrow,
> yet though un-alive,
> our spirits shall dance
> ecstatically,
> the dance of deities adored
> generally,
> by the free world
> we bought with our blood

*In Memoriam of a Modest Shame* is not a bad way to begin. It moralizes and disgruntles. It is sad, angry, honest, evocative, largely sentimental and judgmental. It is messy and leaves a large room for improvement both in the areas of thought and quality of craft, and art allows all these things--the imperfect landmarks which an artist would look back at in the future and say, that is where I started and this is where I am and ahead is a space to improve on.

**Ebenezer Agu** is a poet and nonfiction writer based in Kano State, Nigeria. He studied English and Literature at the University of Nigeria, Nsukka. He is the chief editor of **20.35** *Africa: An Anthology of Contemporary Poetry.*

# In Memoriam of a Modest Shame

# In the Beginning...

## Gory

No glorious beginning,
middle packed with tears and yearning;
unfulfilled dreams, broken hearts,
empty stomachs, fallen comrades.

This land is sick. It has engulfed us
like rats, leaving just skeletons.
Shadows of our pre-being, we became,
trudging along, in modest shame.

The denouement holds no hopes,
mooring on a brand new day, a  dead end.
The sun will not rise again. No hope, no
glories.

The beginning foreshadowed the end.

# The First Sin

Dimly lit concave,
solid walls to wade off all intruders.
Sanctuary of sanctuaries,
abode of those who must never be rivaled.
Two statues of large-horned pigs adorned
the entrance.

The third of the Godhead sometimes,
roams the surface of the earth in gleeful
un-inhibition
the earth and all in it, His plaything.

Bored of trifling with the minds of pigs
and cows,
they agreed:
"let us make us toys in our image and
likeness."

Male and female they were made,
puppets warned at inception,
"dare not see the light;
"dare not be like us!"

They obeyed,
infants, starry-eyed

In the afternoon the Serpent came
raspy-voiced and talked away,
of wonders unseen, a world unexplored.
Both listened,
the female's spirit aroused;
her inner eyes opened to
enormous possibilities.

At night she led the man by the hand
and pointed out the light in the distant
shore.

The Voice called in the morning:
"Adam! Adam! Why have you sought
to be like us?"

So out of Eden they were chased,
for seeking the light.

**Then evil comes home to roost**

# Death at the Door

Closer than David and Jonathan we were,
friends, closer than brothers anywhere.
Freely, we shared everything,
yes, everything, except one thing
which I would not for all the world part.
Yet that never made us drift apart.
That one thing, is my wife
who if any touched, I'll move in with a knife,
and send the person's soul straight to hell,
for early would have tolled the person's bell.

Together we played and made the world
envious, and to split us, they tried all means
devious, but together we stuck like egrets to
cows even when we were hunted like hogs.
We flourished like palm-trees
and bore fruits all days of all seasons
like the biblical river-side trees.

Until in envy, they moved in,
hips wriggling with abandon in sin,
as they ecstatically proclaimed Jeho

Sweet smelling incense on oceans burned,
to sweeten the air for Jeho,
and wide they cast their nets
and very many fishes,
inside they drew.
And so their fold grew,
as they rained their prophecies
on many innocent souls,
beguiling them with prophecies of fear;
Hark! Death at the door, dear.

Graves we see, in front, besides
and behind you.
Run to our sanctuary and hide.
So they waded in and took my man,
with prophecies of how in a day or
two he would die,
and how his friends would make him
insane.
He never for once thought it could be a lie,
but believed with his whole heart, soul and
body,
all the many fearful things they said.
So he quivered and feared the world like never
did anybody, because to him anybody could
have made him dead.

7

That was how they turned a once brave man,
into a frightened and cowering squirrel.
Let the world then burn to the last man,
nothing in the world will ever again be normal.

## To Jeho With Love

With tremulous steps,
we hurry to church.
Clutching in our palms,
naira notes, our offerings to God.

At the church entrance
stands a man with decayed eyes,
begging for alms,
and as we pass him,
we clutch our notes tighter,
lest they fall off our palms,
and be picked by the beggar by the corner.
Oh! They are our offerings to God!

*In the night,*
*Oswald Mtshali called;*
*Son, there is no God above,*
*God is that beggar by the street corner.*

## Chaos

A break away from my cocoon,
slimy paths; a tunnel of
slime, blood and fluffy walls.
Dragged out by
semi hard palms wrapped in white.
Bitten by stinging cold air,
I refused to cry.

Chaos,
society in confusion,
values undefined,
chasing diverse gods,
purpose unclear.
Allah akbar here;
halleluyah there.
Unsure beings,
killing one another here,
tomorrow jettisoning beliefs there.

Scenes I see prepare me for the future,
foisted hypocrisy prime point of nurture.
Deranged beings, truces called
on hypocritical holy days.

Tomorrow we resume…
Misguided folks,
chasing alien gods
whose ways nor languages,
they truly do not understand.

And the bloodshed and confusion
tragically continue…

## Satan's Plea

Misjudgment,
Lucifer's condemnation premature.
His evil pales,
in comparison to man's.

Murderers,
killers of kith and kin;
killers with nukes and words;
killers with pills and injections,
and worse,
the insane murder of
the unwanted child,
carried in the womb for nine full months,

now;
wrapped in plastic,
thrown into a trash can,
the hope of a nation
asphyxiated.

Dark hours, twilight days,
hell stutters, Lucifer enraged…
'Father', he prayed
'Do let this cup pass over me,
for I'm not worthy,
to be called Satan.

## Season's Craze

Countdown: Thirty days to D-day.
Festivity smells thick and strong.
Breath quickens and the heart beats faster,
Santa Claus comes!

Everywhere,
green leaves turn brown.
A misty blanket envelope the world
and everyday,
morning smiles from the
choking grasp of a hot-cold night.
The lazy worker held back in bed,
by the chilly winds of the harmattan.

The craze to make the celebration great,
many times leads to extremes.
Twelve gauge shot guns are dusted,
then highways turn to war-ways,
running slugs finding homes in vulnerable
chests.

Bags of money forcefully taken,
by robbers desirous of a grand season
yet many never live to see the D-day.

The kings of the road inflate fares,
and in a bid to make more money,
drivers turn crazy to their death.
The accelerator is weighed down
with huge stones.

The soul's killed with hemp and akpeteeshi.
Broken bones and mangled flesh,
become relics of this craze.

The *ogas* withhold salaries,
of workers in desperate need.
Fraud turns second nature
and treasuries are rifled
with forged cheques wielded by smart brains.

The body hawker is at her season,
too late she realizes,
the ritual killer needs money for the season.

Frenzied actions.
Everybody desires the meal ticket,
focus though myopic:
it's all for a grand season,
then souls are lost in unreason.

The earth spins round and round and round,
and D-day finally arrives.
Then attention changes,
and all monies accumulated begin duties.
New extensions for new hairdos,
laces and shoes for changed outlook.
Cows, goats and fowls are scrambled for
by those who ordinarily could not afford them.

New cars and refurbished houses
decorate the landscape, then, the craze of
who'd outdo the other in donations
that constitute the numerous ceremonies.
The festivities are many times uncountable,
and for each we must represent.
More money is not made this time
spend and spend is all there is.

The year's pregnancy finally due for delivery,
to the labour room she walked.
The world waited on bated breath,
all churches filled to the brim.
Hosanna, shouted by hearts pious,
as pastors preach for a new life this new season.

The midwife of the year conscientiously
tends the intending mother.
As the warm air turns freezing,
the expectant mother pushes fiercely.
Then, the thundering shouts of
'happy new year!'
herald the birth of the new child.

We pause in our crazy actions,
our breath slowed and our heartbeats normal.
Stocktaking:
what did we gain from this craze?

Epiphany! We realize that,
we lost all and gained nothing,
except a year closer to our graves.
Then we commence the New Year---
disconsolate.

The  year's pregnancy finally due for delivery,
to the labour room she walked.
The world waited on bated breath,
all churches filled to the brim.
Hosanna, shouted by hearts pious,
as pastors preach for a new life this new season.

# The Tragedy of Man

Conceived in darkness,
mother lying on tattered mats,
father sweating it out between thighs,
in a hut where the room floods,
when the heavens weep.

My lot was cast,
among the neglected and impoverished lot,
where abject poverty is the garb of humans.

*Mucus rains from the nostrils of children,*
*protruding belly fed fat with hunger,*
*flies competing violently*
*to lick the mucus from the nostrils.*
*Women with bodies decorated with veins,*
*have their fingers worn rough from*
*scratching arid lands for food*
*and with half-fed stomachs, sleep weary each night.*

*But thought hungry and deprived we were,*
*when the moon casts its beam,*
*on our impoverished village,*
*children dance in frenzy shouting onwa apuo!*
*While the old sit together in harmony drinking gin,*

*and laughing off all the worries in the world.*
*At bedtime although sleeping on tattered mats,*
*we snored away in freedom, unwary of robbers.*

As a juvenile weary of the life,
which the drudgery of poverty promised,
the glow of the metallic city with streetlights
and tarred roads, became my desire. Sitting in
posh cars and apartments, with pockets full of
meal tickets filled my dream.
Dreams! I chased them committed,
out to end my life of drudgery with a deft
stroke.
Adieu to peace of mind, if that was what it
meant.

To attain fame and fortune, I played foul.
Brothers were remorselessly duped and robbed.
Evil became my garb and vehicle to fortune.
Dedicated to the struggle, I got what I sought
too soon; metallic city, a garland of roses for
you!
Wash me clean of the dregs of poverty,
and my cracked, dehydrated skin,
freshen with ointment!

Yet in my gargantuan house,
sleep flies from my eyes.
I am a bank to rob for the marauders
of the night!
While brothers angered at my duplicity,
in vengeance hire assassins to cut me down.
The gardens harbouring well manicured
flowers, in irony portend danger to me,
as assassins could lurk in them and get me
killed.
Ah! The lost freedom of my impoverished
village!

Oh seer, unknot the knotted ropes of my life,
and tell me, what it is that I really want,
what do I desire; what does man desire?
Is it peace of mind and closeness with nature,
or a very firm grasp on mammon
although the worship of him deprives us of
peace?

The voice comes swiftly not waiting,
The answer, ready to give:

Not content with what he has,
is the tragedy of man.

## Under the Guise of Christianity

He goes to church every Sunday,
clothed in all forms of exaltations,
second only to the priest. There,
they preach purity of heart,
to be Christian is to be Christ like, pure.

His heart is filled with
tangible darkness stone-hard.
Darkness cooked with jealousy, greed
and a consuming hatred,
for genius, for he feels inferior,
when geniuses are lauded and
he's neglected.

Then, crush, crush the threats!
The only way for him to feel superior,
is by casting all geniuses into the lake of fire.

## *Otiin Growing in the Desert

Like a cricket's sole shrill,
breaking the night's tranquility,
the alarm shrilled, piercing the
night's stillness, and my soul's sojourn,
with flippant minstrels of the dreamland,
snapped in violence, teeth knocking together
from cold.
Struggle! Eyes *appoloic* red from
poring relentlessly over voluminous books.

In dilapidated classrooms,
with scarce chairs and floors coloured in
broken tiles, windowpanes lost to vandals
and burglary proofs nonexistent,
naked wires protruding from,
where before, sockets stayed,
ceilings caving into cage-like classrooms,
I sit with stomach half-fed and
brain sharpened by desire and dulled by
hunger.

I struggle alone,
no love; no rest.
Dumped amidst thorns,
reaching to the sun almost impossible.
Stuck in this gloom that
choke yet turn me out,
under extremely difficult conditions.
Half-cooked despite all my struggles.

And like *Otiin*
growing in the desert,
I come out with pale leaves.

*\*Scent leaf. A very precious plant among the Obuohians*

## Tattoo Tears

Guns bark everywhere.
I bend low, my eyes focused,
straight on the meal ticket.
No fear, my heart is stout,
solid as Olumo Rock.
I dive like a fish,
scuttle brothers,
and win the struggle.
Cash, reward for hook and crook moves.

I rest not content,
guns aimed at my head bark,
spitting fire and brimstone.
Vengeance moves by angry brothers.
I weep at night,
no peace, no rest, tomorrow I may die,
hazards of life crooked.
No questions, no regrets, for living how I live;
there is no other alternative.

At night I only shed,
tattoo tears.

## Death Ward

The cloth is soaked by
blood flowing from
the mutilated body of,
a man, reduced to a bleeding piece of earth,
by the actions of reckless drivers.

"To the hospital! To the hospital!"
The voices of concerned citizens croaked.
A Good Samaritan provides a car,
and the bleeding piece of earth is whisked off.

White walls, nurses dressed in white.
White sheets, a sea of whiteness,
as if one is among angels and,
the bleeding earth is carried in.

The dumb receptionist,
having extracted a compulsory card fee,
indifferently points to a room.
the bloodied  form is wheeled in.

"Doctor! Doctor!!"
The god does not hear,
he is busy fondling the breast of
a nurse in skimpy gown.

Blood flows out,
breath flies away from,
the bleeding piece of earth,
and the doctor climaxes,
in an office with table for bed.

Then,
frenzied efforts at,
attending to the dead form.
Scissors, surgical blades, stethoscopes,
gloves, and all, are hurriedly gathered.

All actions are late!
The soul flew away,
to meet its creator,
where at least it shall
"Rest in Peace?"

## Demise of the Towncrier

The towncrier is dead,
broken our gourds of tears,
raining like pebbles in a pebble war.

The towncrier is dead!
Why did he die?
The towncrier is dead,
Does he deserve his fate?

The towncrier is dead!
Broken, our gourds of tears,
raining like dews on a cold
December morning.

The towncrier who reported how
the  Elephant traffics in drugs.
The towncrier who said
the Elephant did bad,
in squandering the nation's resources.

The towncrier is dead!
Does he deserve his fate?

The towncrier who said
our lord the Elephant,
Should not impose himself,
on an unwilling populace.

The towncrier who was to reveal
that condemned Omaonwea,
had received hidden clemency,
because she lies on her back
for the Elephant's services.
And for the towncrier's troubles,
the Elephant sent him a letter.

The towncrier is dead
through a letter bomb.
Gene is dead,
for serving us well
in his grave he lies,
together with his bell.

Empty, our gourds of tears.

Karma! Karma!
Catch up with the Elephant,
and post him like a letter,
to his grave!

## Oddiri

Oddiri, ah Oddiri my sister,
the tears rain from my lachrymal glands.
Evil has beset us greatly,
and the good old days lost so soon.
What world of innocence we did have,
fantasy suffusing our hearts with joy,
our future built on hopes,
as we dreamt of a world that greatly needed us.

How we dreamt of journeys to Mars,
living like giants in a world we bettered.
Those days of innocence
when fantasy fired hope
and happiness was derived from dreams.
The days we watched cartoons,
and lived like fairies in a fairyland.
What bliss we did have then,
as we had dreams of affluence and fame,
passionately building hopeful castles,
discovered too soon to be built in the air.

Not that we didn't work hard Oddiri,
but the world bears no goodness for anyone.
Now harsh realities have stripped us of all
we had, as we realize too late,
that much more than bare ability leads to
success here.

Oddiri, our brothers had great plans;
blood was to be their brick.
Our shoulders meant to bear,
the staggering weight of
their mansion of misuse and misrule.
Aha! Humans as pillars!
Pillars alone? No Oddiri,
others were meant to serve as carpets.
The more honoured, elevated,
to solid steps to the top of
this staggering tower of Babel
which God seems to have forgotten.

Oddiri,
here was paradise,
honey flowed, milk sang,
in the Niger River.
We saw them Oddiri, we tasted them too,
and they were communally shared.

Then, who knew,
that milk can be canned?
Who knew, that honey can be prepared,
and together with the canned milk,
sold and money stuffed,
into the pockets of a few brothers?

Brothers?
The very sound of that word,
makes me feel I have blasphemed!
Traitors seem a more appropriate word,
but I must hold it back,
before my head becomes an ornament,
flamboyantly displayed on a pole,
a shouting deterrent to others,
audibly saying; "keep your mouths shut!"
That's another one Oddiri;
you talk only when you are asked to,
and then, say the evils are….
I cannot ever say the word.

But you know sister,
that this is how it is,
with other lands we call developed.
Deep potholes are trademarks,
of roads well constructed!
Well tarred roads are signs of,

living in hell.
This is heaven, heaven on earth, so drum!
Who says electricity must hold on
uninterrupted?
Taking it and bringing it, shows people are
at work!

Fuel scarcity only shows,
that we are thrifty.
We do not waste things here,
we save them for our children.
If we use up all the fuel,
which one will our children use tomorrow?
You say people suffer during this scarcity?
Is it not only the greedy ones that suffer?
The non-greedy ones manage the nothing,
which they have.

You want me to say it, don't you know?
This is Africa, where kola is given,
from the bottom of our hearts,
to influence service.
Although our forefathers gave kolas
to welcome and show appreciation
and not as a necessity for deliverance of service.

Hush! Oddiri let no one hear it;
they eliminate oppositions here,
to sustain their bloody rule.
The schools are barren,
of implements of production.
Teachers starved, left, as they are, hungry.
They are donkeys, mules of work.
If they protest,
schools are shutdown.
When they are tired of protesting,
they continue the sacrifices.

Tell me Oddiri, what does our big brother
sacrifice?
Hush baby, we know it, but
let the knowledge die with us!
If the poor man is fed up,
let him pick up his gun and go rob.
When you let the fool,
he turns the gun on a man poorer.
The land reeks of violence, is it not only in the
slums?

The poor are like hounds,
locked up in a common pen,
tearing up one another.

While in skyscrapers and posh cars,
children of the same mother,
sip champagne and set fire,
on the congested dog pens.

Ah, Oddiri, evil reigns here.
Tell me sister, is it true?
Did we ever have a good time?
Was there ever a time,
when all was good and well?
Wake me up with a slap, Oddiri,
maybe my memory fails me.
And like a man suffering from amnesia,
I begin to wonder;
did our fathers ever live
a life of freedom and equality?
Is this our great land of Iduu,
where all was once good and everybody
merry?

## Deserted Mother

Mother, when my gaze falls on you,
painful pangs hit my heart,
and my eyes are filled with tears,
at what I see;

Your eyes are like the owl's,
stuck in sunken sockets,
in a head adorned with,
pale and falling hairs.

Your ribs are visible to eyes,
many miles away.
Your flat belly, merges with your back,
a perfect drawing of the human skeleton!

You are hypertensive,
caused by
many fearful thoughts of abandonment,
and posses a 'locking waist',
inherited from,
climbing hilly roads to farms,
even when you are heavy,
with age.

African queen, I see your
once glittering dark complexion,
turned muddy-brown from
long exposure to the sun,
when your body is covered with dust,
soaked in sweat.

Mother,
your breast suckled many sons,
who today wine and dine,
with the greatest of the land.
Are your woes not over now?

But impetuous sons –your children--
have forgotten and abandoned,
the womb that bore them,
the breast that suckled them.
And abandoned,
you remain desolate.

## Wonderland.

My land is a land of wonders.

It was so simple,
like games by kids,
a simple counting,
of eligible voters.
At the final count we had:
forty voters.

The drums rolled for the elections.
Four contestants danced to the arena,
conspicuous among them, the incumbent.
At the final count he won,
the incumbent won,
with a staggering eighty votes!

## For Flora, Fauna

The choking sobs of
flora and fauna,
being driven to extinction.
*Azu* begs to breathe,
*Ofirima* struggles to live
*Ejanla* battles for survival
the hyenas no longer laugh,
laughter has died in them,
as hot leads from greedy men,
find homes in their hearts.

Minks and anacondas grow extinct,
as snakeskin shoes and fur coats,
become the *in-thing*.
The mighty elephant,
is dispossessed of its tusk
Kurtz needs ivory for profit.
Deforestation outweighs afforestation,
and the natural canopy of trees,
is lost in wanton destruction.

Here and there,
the urine of profit factories,
render aquatic habitats desolate,

and once profitable and fertile lands,
turn to deserts in broad daylight.
Submerged shrubs fighting
scaly land rinds,
products of oil companies.

Children are bequeathed with cancerous cells,
as irritant fumes envelope the sphere.
Life stops. Brothers, this is death, this is the end.
All life is submerged,
in the chthonic world of
man's controllable excesses.

They grow hoarse,
the praying voices,
the choking sobs of flora and fauna,
that desperate plea of plants and animals,
the hoarse voices begging and beseeching,
that they may be allowed to live again.

*Fishes of all sizes

## Martyr for Fatherland

He strides,
sure and confident,
except that,
he sways,
when the wind blows.

He dresses,
always so immaculately,
with,
an indigo khaki shirt,
and,
bell-bottom brown trousers.
Except that,
the shirt is faded
and the trousers, threadbare,
testimony to protracted usage.

From his mouth jumps,
big words,
opprobrious, obnoxious
obfuscate, oscillate.
He is learned, and very well too.

He is the brain of the cartel,
he is not the head of the cartel.
He is the engine room of the cartel,
he is not the moneybag of the cartel.
He is the overworked and over starved one,

*He never complains, the good one.*
*He sways and faints,*
*and falls, cold.*

The doctor summoned,
the post-mortem performed;
then "he's dead", he proclaimed
the reason; "insufficient nutrients."

## Soloist for the State

*The land is green,*
*it's green for me.*

Even in the marshes,
we could hear her voice,
knifing through
our consciousness,
dragooning feelings of
patriotism from
those who have been
purged clean of such feelings.

TY,
soloist for the state,
I marvel!
I marvel at the prompts,
to your sonorous melody,
portraiture of what is not.

I look around, even
in this marshland,
the grasses have become brown.

I face the streets,
pot-bellied children,
stagger around on
broomstick legs.

I turn further,
see the graduates,
the whimpering soles of their shoes,
scrapped to the leather,
as they trudge the streets,
in search of non-existent jobs.

*The land is green,*
*it's green for me.*

I find greenness,
in vacant ghostlike eyes
of the millions trudging the streets.
I seek greenness,
in the hemp-reddened eyes of the youths,
pushed to crimes.
All that stares back at me,
are pale brownness and redness.

*The land is green*
*it's green for me.*

In the posh residences of
the demonized exploiters,
green shrubs are flowers.
Well-fed children,
bounce around like
green ping-pong.
Ornately dressed wives,
shuffle around in
green agbadas,
and in the wallets of them all,
the green dollar is the legal tender.

TY,
soloist for the state,
what was your motivation?
State-day performances?

## Breathtaking Imperfections

First class brains,
streets populated with them,
flaunting certificates, useless,
plus innate knowledge practical,
but unrecognised

Tightfisted bourgeois;
alienated job opportunities,
reserved for own kids born and unborn,
capitalism overblown; nauseous
grab-and-keep philosophy elevated.
Who do you know? Who don't you know?
Keys to haven.

You could trudge to the Sahara,
build sand dunes, clamber atop,
to reach the top and maybe sunlight.
Slight wind, and you are on the floor:
no foundations.
Pack the sand, feed on them,
who cares?

Hollow eyes witnessing a party,
the favoured few, on *Owambes,*

overfed. Toothpicks in mouths,
dogs too, fed fat with flesh,
now reject bones.
Leftovers go sour, thrown away.

First class brains, crawl in dustbins,
vultures competing.
Some days, vultures feed too
on first class brains' corpses.

Hollow-eyed pleas, unheeded.
Gentle songs of plea,
didn't make them yield.

Clangs on empty sardine tins,
music violent, tempo risen.
They glanced at them, and looked away.
Then one day, hunger and anger fired
desperation, bread knives came in handy,
well-fed guts were carved apart,
all energy used.

Denouement.

The vultures came in the evening,
and held a huge feast.

## The Cursed

I am the child born into want,
clothed in malnourishment.
Even as an infant,
my crown of glory was want.

I am he, who to school,
trudged round dusty streets,
hawking wares, boiled groundnuts and others,
dressed in brownish white singlets,
and oversize rainbow-colour shorts.

No hopes of university education,
it is a dream unrealised in my lineage,
the future could only be accessed,
with the key of apprenticeship,
to slave merchants domiciled in Gabon.

I'm fate's punching bag:
perfect example of
generational poverty,
no need to dream of a rosy future,
the future I know is the food in my belly.

## Mad World

My mind is a dump of filth they say,
"Dirt only you conjure", some bray.

I see it, you see it, don't you?
The father,
turning the infant child to pounded yam,
a vigorous pounding away,
in fulfillment of
the ritual demands
of an insatiable goddess.

These are our children,
are they not?
These skimpily clad ones,
flaunting their wares
On the streets of Rome, London, and Ikeja,
venereal diseases shared with the willing.
Children we birthed but failed to nurture.

In the creeks and hinterland,
their amnesty has failed.
Enraged youths,
with focus solely on enrichment,
still wield guns menacingly,

another form of armed robbery,
name changed to kidnapping.

We have been left fatherless,
not even a surrogate one appointed.
*Mamatura* in frenzy,
inspired by power lust and cash desires,
hid away a corpse in Mohammed's holy land.
Now the land is in confusion,
our destination uncertain.

Tears drop, where are the caskets?
Bombed and grenaded into bits,
vultures are now friends,
functional caskets to these soldiers,
slain on the streets of
Tripoli, Benghazi, Cairo,
Abidjan, and even Damascus.

At Suleja,
the youthful investments
of many a toiling parent,
khaki and white vest clad,
are bombed into smithereens
by power drunk politicians,
besieging the electoral house.

Through these dark paths,
where experiences are my eyes.
Through these slippery paths of amazonic
forests,
I feel my way to tomorrow,
learning of man's frailties,
yet seeking a sane world,
but finding none.

This is the apocalypse I rant,
they say 'shut up, you ant!'
I see all, I say all!
Oruh, the oracle, towncrier like Okigbo.
Yet they say I'm mad.
But it's not I who am mad,
it's the whole world
that has gone to the marketplace naked.

## Nature's Children

I claw desperately at
persistent visions,
real, heart rending,
genocidal hurls
at nature, her children,
and allies.

Flora and fauna's cries,
petitions for survival,
sent to drilling masters,
who for profit can destroy the world.
Petitions on deaf ears,
vegetation destroyed.

From the dusty and desert-like zone,
rises another cry,
ominous, cancerous,
masquerading as Haram,
which like the locust,
gradually eats us up.

Deeply pockmarked faces are tell tales,
askew limbs enforce the menaces,
and death strolls casually through the streets,

nature's children brutally vandalized,
pictures reminiscent
of apocalypse, imminent.

I weep for nature's children,
those who rise East of the Niger,
six year old hustlers,
who for food and fees roam the streets,
hawking trays of goods:
infant-bread-winners.

A moment of silence please,
for the brave child-soldiers,
warriors who roamed the streets
of war-torn Africa,
warriors who totter with guns,
several inches taller than them.

This dreary world makes me teary,
nature's begotten now weary.
Wearied by repeated tragedies.

Yet I totter on,
a participant chronicler,
victim of maladies,
past, present, and futuristic,
gnawing  away at our existence .

## One Billion Rising

Even from the womb I was scarred.
Your viper-tongue, spitting venomous
hateful words on mother--
hot iron rods piercing my heart.
You pummelled her with your fists,
blows that I received too.
It wasn't mother's fault
that my sex was female.
Not your problem, you wanted a son.
If I knew I would have conjured up a penis.
You did not know?
Infant hands can sculpt a penis,
and replace the vagina with it.

You rated Obi and Emeka over me,
slave-daughter, maid to my brothers.
Nobody ever questioned that,
Mother, a willing ally to that injustice.
I never saw Bereton,
you gave me Ozuoba Primary.

Who trains a girl? I stopped at elementary.
Bereton was for my brothers,
boys, who deserve higher education.

My dream was to be a doctor,
generous father, you trained me to be
a seamstress to increase my bride price.

A seamstress married off to
Ojo, beast of a man.
When his turgid member is not abusing me,
his fist and all he can grab
rains on me.
The pockmarks on my body,
are testaments to his manliness.
That puppy of a man,
who flees, when a fellow man
challenges him at the arena.
Warrior at home; coward outside,
stingy at home; king of the pubs

At his death,
his *umunna* and *umuada*,
blamed me for his demise,
bathed him, and gave me the water to drink.
My head still bears scars,
relics of the ferocious
shaving of my hair by the *umuada*,
with a semi-blunt *aguba*

I have drank full,
from this river of bitterness!
My sex is not a crime,
I shall stand up!
From afar, the sounds of drums come,
sisters(and brothers)being roused into action,
and like vexed cobras, we shall strike,
hands interlinked across seas and borders,
a billion of us, rising menacingly.

## Victims Too

We have fought battles fiercer than this,
crushing thick skinned soldiers under our feet.
Fear clogged the minds of the bravest,
soldier-kings, we were feared, I bet you.

At home though,
one bark from her and you scurry in like a rat.
Love has weakened your heart at the edges,
and you became a "coward" for her.

Tomorrow she will walk away and you'll
find another,
and rule the world, but not your home.

## I Am Not Your Son Anymore

I stayed on the path you set me on mother.
The Master Pastor-is-always-right road.
I am your son, favoured and all, remember?

Master Pastor reminded me daily too,
of, Miriam, Moses, and leprosy,
a homily on how,
God always takes sides
with the anointed.

But Satan will not let me be,
always whispering rebellious questions
in my ears:
where do your tithes go to?
Why is Master Pastor getting fatter,
while your flesh is drying up?

Master Pastor says no questions,
and pointed me to;
Miriam, Moses, and leprosy.
Mighty men have been destroyed, he said,
for asking questions like that.

But he never said,
how mighty men have been caged by that story,

commanders of thousands tethered to a
man's whims,
like sheep following a shepherd,
an image conveniently woven into the
Holy Book.

Mother, am I still your son?
The questions are sprouting branches
in my brain,
poking holes in the cocoon of my beliefs.
Maybe it is Satan's still small voice,
or plain reason seeking clarification.

Why is our society filled with so much evil,
when churches sprout daily, from all nooks
and crannies?
Why does the Pastor preach;
"Be your brother's keeper" on Sunday,
and on Monday, evict his brother,
who is also his tenant?

"Remember Miriam, Moses and leprosy!"
Master Pastor bellowed--an effort on his part,
as sound struggled out of fat cheeks and a fat
neck.
I remember too when Master Pastor was as thin
as me,

when he owned no houses or flashy cars.
"The Lord is good" is only for him,
I'm dry as the Sahara, in pocket and in flesh.

Miriam, Moses and leprosy!
Master Pastor's scam expression to
steal my possession.
Maybe it is Satan again whispering things
to me,
but to be coerced into blind servitude, I see,
is to chain one's soul to a burning house.

I am sorry mother,
but I will not be your son anymore,
if being tied to dogma
makes you my mama.
This son you birthed is a free soul,
giving equal chance to 'Satan' and Master
Pastor's Jesus.
May he who best answers my questions take
my soul.

## This War Will Consume You

I am the one you declared war on;
...brought your armoured vehicles,
mercenaries and assault rifles.

You stood on a podium built of quicksand,
and fired shots at me.

I had a shield you never knew of--
a wise man hides a few things,
even from those from the same bloodline.

I remained quiet; no shots from my side,
my army fuming, like rabid dogs begging
to be unleashed.

Yesterday,
you were still thumping your chest,
your eyeballs blazing fire,
your face gnarled in anger.

The world remembers
(even if you have amnesia),
that with these hands,
I built you from scratch.
Your success solely my efforts.

I'm not the type you rain hot coals on
and he cowers.
I'm the Lion-King, battle ready.
When your bullets have long stopped
landing on my shield,
and a truce you solicit,
then shall I roll out my nuclear arsenals.
And this war will consume you.

# In Memoriam of a Modest Shame

Alhamdulillah!
Halleluyah to the god!

The chants of the praise singer
could not elicit any response.

The multitude of sheepish followers
bleary eyed and hunger ravaged,
stayed mute.
Hunger had drained the fuel
for above-the-din "Sai Babas."

Alhamdulillah!
Halleluyah to the Messiah!

Placed on a scale,
side by side with humans,
the worth of the moo-moos
outweighed those of humans.
Cowland, with a Cowmander-in-Herds,
blood drowned the voices:
sickles severed carotids,
heads of infants split in halves,
limbs and hearts of adults cut off--
the sickle is not a respecter of age.

Alhamdulillah!
Sai Baba the King!

A deadhead at the helm,
fiery fire of indifference in his eyes.
He watches, unseeing
as hunger ravages his subjects,
and death prowls his kingdom.

Fate, all knowing,
let the fools, place a sceptre in the hands
of a Messiah exposed as a fraud.

## Purgatory

They won't let me sleep;
these demons.
Each with its skeletal hand,
clawing away at what remains,
of my sanity.

I have hit rock bottom,
levitation impossible.
My feet stuck
at the junction of
now and the hereafter.

Scrawny thoughts;
decapitated bodies,
naked and emaciated,
completing a cauldron
of blood.

This is where we inhabit,
now that Hope's head
has been gruesomely
chopped off--
at the junction of
wakefulness to a daring reality,
and a lustful wish for an
unknown eternity.

## Apocalypse

Pattering on roofs
like defiant horse hoofs.
Whirlwind,
deafening thunderclaps,
dark night seared by
the brightest of lightning,
harbingers of the deluge.
The heavens opened,
sheaths of rain, linking up with
other sheaths 'raining' from underneath.

Tarred streets turned to streams–
at the beginning–and gradually
dry land turned to rivers,
bungalows submerged,
tall trees and six storey buildings
next in line.

Oceans, seas and rivers
have merged,
plants and animals submerged.

Underneath the deluge,
where I battle for breath,
a waterproof Holy Book floats,

and my mind races back to:
and God spake unto Noah…
neither shall all flesh
be cut off any more
by the waters of a flood.

# Interlude

## The Mourners

We wail inconsolably, gnashing our teeth,
twisting our hairs and rolling in the mud.
"This death is unbearable;
this loss irreparable."
But our attitude does not,
in the slightest of ways,
befit that unbearable loss.

Let us start by
cutting our bodies
with knives.
So that bathed in blood,
we shall have, in the right way,
started the mourning
befitting an irreparable loss.

And to sum it up,
let us take axes,
and hack down each other
so that dead,
we shall have proven,
that our loss,
was truly unbearable!

## American Lady

My American lady won't let me sleep,
Nor read, or tweet or Facebook at least.
She is at it at odd hours with vids,
photos and voice notes,
of the incredibility of America:

"Hey, do you know here rain doesn't
fall on people?
It makes a detour just before their bodies
and goes to the drains."
For me, a new wonder to imagine and
long for, maybe in vain.
"Here, cars stop abruptly for you to pass,"
she says,
"unlike your Africa where bikes crush
you on the sidewalks."

She was in "Africa" two weeks ago.
Born and bred, she lived here all her life.
But like the outsider, who weeps
louder than the bereaved,
Nigeria has become Africa, and Africa a
country.

"See the beauty of the world," she says,
showing me a video of a waterfall in a hotel.
I note that the accent has changed--a mixture
of Indian and Puerto Rican slur.
I exclaim in wonder, unsure of a reason.

My American lady says I must learn Spanish
before I come, and then rattles off
"por qué no dijiste nada."
How America became a Spanish country my
backwardness won't let me know,
but I agreed with her, the agama lizard
nodding in assent.

Oh America, land of wonders and abrupt
change:
you made me a new lady, an American lady,
but couldn't make yourself a perfect Trump.

## The Poet

Words that come from you,
perverse definition of me,
a man, whose soul you know not.
You call me *Jadum*,
tell the world my hair is *dada,*
yet I feed not from dustbins.
I walk not the streets naked!
You think I care?
Say what you want!

Ideas take flight,
I grow wings too,
and like Agbor witches,
I race after them.
Soliloquizing by the way:
gesturing at unseen beings;
laughing to myself,
as I grab an idea here,
or miss another there.

Muses could be cunning,
unhinging my sanity at will,
and I'm left in a state of
near insanity.
But I know who I am,

I commune not with mortals.
I am friends with gods,
who alone comprehend
the esoteric language I speak.

Call me madman,
call me *Jadum,*
but I'm that seer,
who converses with gods,
in esoteric languages,
incomprehensible to mere mortals.

# Rumination

In the beginning,
our voices were baritone,
peacocking our trade.
Appareled always in white:
white shirts and trousers,
matching white shoes and suits.

We owned the world,
and walked around,
with the swagger
of the nouveau-riche:
patrolling, controlling,
our egos, mountain sized.

Ego reduction was swift.
Dad died, our spirits left.
Accounts dwindled,
our fleshes thinned.
clothes are rags,
peacocking ends.

## Just a Day

Give me one day,just one day,
a day when I dance around in circles,
at the thought of mum,
preparing ukazi soup with achara.

I need a day, just one day,
when Orie ukwu was special,
and the thought of akamu
and akara from yaa Ebere,
meant breakfast was served.

I dream of a day, another day,
when the full moon
meant that my lover, tied up at home,
would take a stroll and meet me,
at Mbaraobom

Give me a day, just a day,
When Christmas scent, would
herald the coming of
distant kith and kin,
not seen for long.

I need a day, but can't find one,
when I can bask in the euphoria of innocence,

devoid of backroom mockery.
All I have now,
Is a world that walks on its head.

Can hope part the curtain of darkness...

## Gems Don't Die

Birth shrills,
sparkling gem the product.

Kindergarten:
infantile innocence
beget a muddling up,
the genesis.
Before the claspy hand
of errant juvenile,
created a collage of
suppressive influences.

Secondary and tertiary days
mirrored a stuttering:
gem has become stone-like.
A quack doctor diagnosed:
sophophobia.

He was a quack.
The world didn't see, I saw.
Hopes died, mine lived.
I fanned the fire, a starting process.
Oddiri took over, using billows

Maturity is a panacea
when mixed with responsibility,
begetting a spring,
washing off mud.

Today the world gathers,
lured by the gem's sparks.
Everybody is curtseying:
kabiyesi.

## Man is God

A time comes when
to your back are the
marauding armies of Pharaoh,
and to your front,
the malevolent Red Sea roaring at the top
of its voice,
and by your sides jungles, harbouring
hungry lions.

Such a time when
sadness cakes, despair
takes root and emptiness
wraps you up in a blanket of discomfort.

I speak of a time when cycles turn full,
when friends become foes,
families turn to strangers,
and the dreams shared
become the nightmares dreaded.

A time when you stretch out,
and no hand links with yours,
and the promise of a tomorrow shared,
becomes a future so bleak .

A time when to rise,
you fall to the bottom,
and from the deepest of quagmires,
you derive strength.

The peeping in of the sun
through tiny holes
activates the chlorophyll,
and like a resilient plant,
you sprout and edge upwards.

Such a time do you realise
that for man,
there is no depth too low,
from which he can never arise.
For he is man, and that is all
he needs to be.

...and usher in a new dawn?

## Revolution

Today,
our bodies are cut into bits,
in the struggle for liberty.
For freedom yet unattainable,
we are labeled corrupt and violent,
while brothers are mauled down daily,
by unrelenting bullets from either sides.

Today,
we go hungry and fight angry,
our fingers worn rough,
with works befitting beasts.
To make for change, the guns we picked.
The braver fought, the less brave clapped.

But tomorrow,
yet though un-alive,
our spirits shall dance ecstatically,
the dance of deities adored generally,
by the free world
we bought with our blood.

## Prophecy

Mouthpiece of the ancestors.
crowned oracle of the gods.
The gods reveal, I proclaim.
Hear brothers, the words of the gods.

Proclaimed by me, with my Ogene immersed,
in the great river of Iyibom that enforces
attention.
The gods are roused, their slumber disrupted
by sacrifices made at their altars.

And the gods congregate--*Kamalu*,
*Ogwuma, Nnemmiri and Egbu*--
and with the oppressed they match,
aha, the battle begins!

To protect selfish interests,
wicked overlords get the head of brothers
bashed,
Ala is stained and cries to Elu;
husband of mine, do you watch this in silence?

Tears' doors, unlocked,
*Elu* weeps an ocean full,

at the altars of all the gods.
Beseeched, the gods dance into battle.

Brothers, the gods rally us,
as we rallied them.
The battle begins,
let our dreams bear fruits.
'*Ise*'!

Okigbo father, elephants are elephants,
Agbada clad or khaki clad!
The battle of enraged peasants and the gods,
is waged against all elephants!

Rendered wretched of the earth,
brothers, Kamalu shall strike through us,
all the gods of the land shall fight with us!
You ask for weapons?
Ofo na Ogu are our weapons.
Okigbo, we're invokers of thunder,
thunder shall strike through us,
and right all injustices.

Now that the gods are roused,
who dare stand before us?
Let the obdurate die,
If he refuses to change his ways--Ise!

Brothers, even the coward who dies many times,
before death finally embraces him,
sometimes wishes for a quick death,
as a glorious relief!
Kamikaze? Then let it be!

But the gods render us invincible.
So up! Up! Brothers, the battle begins.
Even the toothless fowl,
sometimes turns its beak into teeth to
contend with dogs!

I see the gates opened,
brothers tremble on their feet enraged.
My voice hoarse croaks: "throw open!
throw open these gates!"

The gates of profiteering companies,
Imperialist stooges, alienating labour,
overworking the workers, and underpaying
them.
Let Ogwuma stripe them, and if they have ears
let them hear.

*Let Ogwuma bathe them with leprosy,*
*make them whiter than white.*
*If they are repentant, let them go bathe*
*at Iyibom, and they shall be cleansed.*

And the practitioners of the foreign God,
professing one thing, and doing the other,
lead Nnemiri in, to scourge them.
Let them be pregnant, all of them!

*The man-woman steps in,*
*inflicts them with pregnancy.*
*Soon death will greet them,*
*if they fail to change their ways.*

Destroyers of flora and fauna,
children sitting on the fence,
abandoning mother and conniving with
the evil ones. Let Egbu give them warning
stripes!

*Egbu, the great one*
*that cuts and catches*
*drags them on their ears*
*Stripes them with medicinal njujukpata*

The gods advance, from all sides.
Now the royal house alone is left.
Lots are cast and *Kamalu* chosen,
and the great one fumes, trembling on his toes:

Provocation from *Beso Rock*,
builds *Kamalu's* anger,
into dark pregnant clouds.

Intoxicated with fury
Kamalu strikes fiercely,
and Beso Rock is set ablaze.

## Acknowledgement

A million appreciation to my mentor and father, the Odozi Obodo, Rep. Sam Onuigbo FNIM, the man who teaches me daily and empowers me to dare to reach for heights beyond the sky.

You have pushed me to do better, to become better and work smartly. Thank you so much for making me believe that I can still dare. I hope that one day I will finally make you proud.

This first step was made possible by you, your words, your grace and more. God bless you, Dee!

Nnaemeka Oruh studied English at the University of Port Harcourt, Nigeria. Oruh's political essays and poems have appeared in several prints and online journals. Nnaemeka's themes are derived mainly from the point-of-view of a discontented youth, seeking to find meaning in a society of false promises and hopes.

He is currently the Editor-in-Chief of *Ikenga Chronicles*. *In Memoriam of a Modest Shame* is his first collection of poems.

Nnaemeka is a gender and rights advocate who lives in Port Harcourt, Rivers State.

Printed in the United States
by Baker & Taylor Publisher Services

Printed in the United States
by Baker & Taylor Publisher Services